FRANCIS FRITH'S

A TASTE OF GLOUCESTERSHIRE AND THE COTWOLDS

THE FRANCIS FRITH COLLECTION

www.francisfrith.com

FRANCIS FRITH'S

A Taste of

GLOUCESTERSHIRE
& THE COTSWOLDS

Wotton-under-Edge, Long Street 1903 49798

Compiled by Julia Skinner

First published in the United Kingdom by
The Francis Frith Collection in 2012.
Paperback Edition ISBN 978-1-84589-460-3

British Library Cataloguing in Publication Data

A Taste of Gloucestershire & the Cotswolds
Julia Skinner

The Francis Frith Collection®
Oakley Business Park, Wylye Road,
Dinton, Wiltshire SP3 5EU
Tel: +44 (0) 1722 716 376
Email: info@francisfrith.co.uk
www.francisfrith.com

Printed and bound in England
Contains material sourced from responsibly managed forests

Front Cover: Cheltenham, High Street 1901 47265t

The colour-tinting in this image is for illustrative purposes only, and is not intended
to be historically accurate.

CONTENTS

INTRODUCTION

Travel around Gloucestershire and the Cotswolds through the pages of this book and discover a selection of the delicious traditional food of the area, as well as some of the stories and fascinating facts behind the recipes. Your journey will be given added savour by the historical images taken by photographers from The Francis Frith Collection, showing the people and places of Gloucestershire and the Cotswolds in the past.

Regional traditional dishes were developed from the local produce that was available to thrifty housewives who had to feed large, hungry families on a limited budget. Many of the old recipes also reflect the limited cookery techniques that were available in the past, as well as the skills of the cooks who were able to provide cheap and tasty meals with only a fire, a skillet and a cauldron to cook with, often producing the historical version of 'boil in the bag' meals.

This book is not intended to provide a comprehensive collection of the local recipes of the region, and some recipes are modern interpretations using some of the fine local produce that the area is famous for, but we hope that the food described within these pages, as well as the descriptions of traditional customs, sayings and local dialect words, will provide you with a taste of Gloucestershire and the Cotswolds.

Lechlade, The Church from the River c1955 L147057

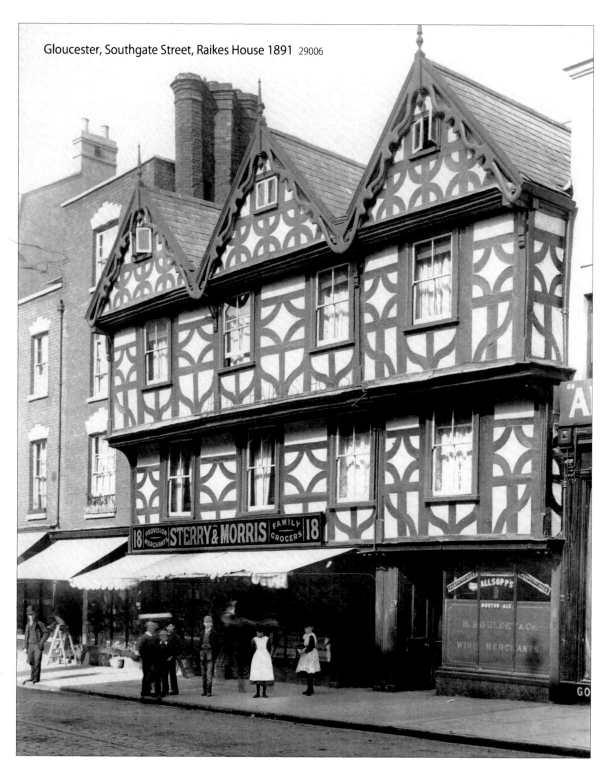

Gloucester, Southgate Street, Raikes House 1891 29006

SOUPS

— . —

RECIPE

— . —

White Foam Soup

This is a light and tasty soup which is traditional to Gloucestershire. This recipe makes enough for about 6 people, so halve the quantities if you want to make less.

1 onion
1 stick of celery
1 clove of garlic
50g/2oz butter
25g/1oz plain flour
1.2 litres/2 pints of milk
A small piece of mace blade
2 eggs, separated
Salt and pepper
50g/2oz finely-grated cheese
1 tablespoonful of chopped fresh parsley

Chop the onion and celery very finely, and crush the garlic. Melt the butter in a large saucepan, stir in the flour and then gradually add the milk, stirring it thoroughly. Bring to the boil, stirring continually, then reduce the heat and simmer for 2 minutes. Add the onion, celery, garlic and blade of mace, and simmer the soup gently at a low heat until it is well flavoured.

Remove from heat and allow to cool slightly, then stir in the beaten yolks of the eggs. Reheat the soup but take care not to allow it to boil. Add salt and pepper to taste, and the grated cheese, still making sure that the soup does not boil.

Whisk or beat the egg whites to a stiff froth, and carefully fold half into the soup using a large metal spoon. Pour the rest of the egg white into a soup tureen or individual soup bowls, and pour the soup over. Sprinkle with the chopped fresh parsley, and serve with crispy fried croutons of bread.

— . —

Cheltenham, High Street 1901 47266

Minchinhampton, The Golf Links, The 3rd Hole 1910 62692

RECIPE

— . —

Sorrel Soup

Common, or Garden, Sorrel is also known as Spinach Dock or Narrow-leaved Dock. It is a perennial herb that is often cultivated as a vegetable, but is also found growing wild. Sorrel has a pleasantly sharp flavour with a lemony tang and makes an excellent soup for the spring or summer. This recipe makes a large quantity, enough for about 8 people.

Sorrel should not be cooked in an aluminium or cast-iron pan, as the natural acids in the plant will react with the metal and affect the flavour.

> 450g/1 lb sorrel leaves
> 2.5 litres/4½ pints chicken stock
> 150ml/ ¼ pint cream
> 75g/3oz butter
> 2 egg yolks
> 1 large onion
> 2 tablespoonfuls of plain flour
> 2 tablespoonfuls of fresh breadcrumbs
> Salt and black pepper

Wash and chop the sorrel. Heat the butter in a saucepan and fry the chopped onion until it is transparent. Add the sorrel and cook for a few minutes to soften it. Sprinkle the flour over the vegetables and mix well, and cook for about 1 minute.

In another saucepan, bring the stock to the boil, then gradually add it to the vegetables, stirring all the time. Add the breadcrumbs, and season to taste. Bring to the boil, stirring continually, then reduce the heat, cover the pan and simmer gently for about 1 hour.

The soup can be liquidized at this stage if a smooth consistency is preferred, before continuing:

Beat the egg yolks with the cream and add a little of the hot soup to the mixture, stirring well, then gradually combine the mixture with the rest of the soup in the pan, stirring well, over heat, but not allowing the soup to boil. Serve with a swirl of extra cream and crispy fried croutons of bread.

— . —

Cirencester, Market Place 1898 40965

RECIPE

— . —

Chestnut Soup

Chestnuts are said to have been introduced to Britain by the Romans. The Gloucestershire area is rich in Roman remains, and there is a saying 'scratch Gloucestershire and find Rome'. The city of Gloucester itself stands on the site of an old Roman fort that was known as 'Glevum', and the Roman town of Cirencester ('Corinium') was one of the most important towns in Roman Britain.

This makes an ideal soup for Christmas time. A tin of chestnut purée can be used if preferred, instead of fresh chestnuts.

> 450g/1 lb chestnuts
> 1.2 litres/2 pints chicken or vegetable stock
> 4 tablespoonfuls cream
> 25g/1oz butter
> ¼ teaspoonful white pepper
> ½ teaspoonful salt
> ½ teaspoonful caster sugar
> A blade of mace

Cut the ends off the chestnuts, and roast them in a moderate oven (180°C/350°F/ Gas Mark 4) for about 20 minutes, until the outer and inner skins will peel off easily. Remove all the skins and then put the chestnuts in a saucepan with the vegetable stock, white pepper, salt, pepper, mace and caster sugar. Simmer all together for 1 hour or longer, until the chestnuts are quite tender.

When the chestnuts are cooked, take out the blade of mace and discard. Rub the chestnuts through a fine sieve (or put through a blender), moistening them with a little of the stock. Rinse out the saucepan, and return the chestnut purée and stock to it. Add the cream, and bring the soup to just below boiling point, stirring well, then reduce the heat, cover the pan and simmer gently for about 20 minutes, until it is quite smooth – it should have the consistency of thin cream, but add a little milk or stock if it is too thick. Check for seasoning, and adjust to taste if necessary.

— . —

FISH

— . —

RECIPE

— . —

Salmon with Cucumber Sauce

Rising 2000 ft (610 metres) above sea level upon the wild slopes of Plynlimon in Wales, the River Severn which flows through north-western Gloucestershire is the longest river in Britain, at 220 miles in length. It was once navigable from where it joins the Bristol Channel to Welshpool, 128 miles up the river from Gloucester. Some of the best salmon is caught in the River Severn, traditionally caught by salmon fishermen using a special net on a Y-shaped frame known as a 'lave net'. Fishermen also used to trap salmon in funnel-shaped baskets placed across the river estuary, but these are rarely seen nowadays. Salmon and trout served with a cream and cucumber sauce is a traditional dish in many parts of England. This is an ideal dish for hot summer days.

1.8kg/4 lbs salmon, gutted and scaled
A small amount of melted butter, for brushing on to the salmon
3 parsley or thyme sprigs
Half a lemon, cut into 2 further segments
1 large cucumber, peeled
25g/1oz butter
115ml/4 fl oz dry white wine
3 tablespoonfuls of finely chopped dill
4 tablespoonfuls of sour cream, or natural yogurt if preferred
Salt and pepper

Pre-heat the oven to 220°C/425°F/Gas Mark 7.

Season the salmon and brush it inside and out with melted butter. Place the herbs and lemon in the cavity. Wrap the salmon in foil, folding the edges together securely, then bake in the pre-heated oven for 15 minutes. Remove the fish from the oven and leave in the foil for 1 hour, then remove the skin from the salmon.

Meanwhile, halve the cucumber lengthways, scoop out the seeds, and dice the flesh. Place the cucumber in a colander, toss lightly with salt, leave for about 30 minutes to drain, then rinse well and pat dry.

Heat the butter in a small saucepan, add the cucumber and cook for about 2 minutes, until translucent but not soft. Add the wine to the pan and boil briskly until the cucumber is dry. Stir the dill and sour cream or yogurt into the cucumber. Season to taste and serve immediately with salmon.

— . —

RECIPE

— · —

Salmon Baked in Pastry

900g/2 lbs fillet of salmon
Salt and pepper
Lemon juice
1 tablespoonful olive oil
675g/1½ lbs puff pastry
225g/8oz onions or shallots
Half a teaspoonful chopped fresh tarragon
115g/4oz button mushrooms
1 egg, beaten, for glazing the pastry

Oven temperature: 190°C/375°F/Gas Mark 5.

Season the salmon with salt, pepper and lemon juice. Heat the olive oil in a large frying pan and lightly fry the salmon on both sides. Take the salmon out of the pan and leave to cool.

Roll out the puff pastry on a floured surface to form an oblong shape large enough to enclose the salmon. Chop the onions or shallots very finely, and sweat them in the pan the fish was cooked in, together with the tarragon. Allow to cool, then spread over one half of the pastry. Thinly slice the mushrooms and place them on top of the onions. Season with salt and pepper.

Place the salmon on top of the vegetables, fold over the other half of the pastry to enclose it all, and seal the edges. Place, folded side down, on a well-greased baking sheet and brush the top with beaten egg to glaze. Bake in the pre-heated oven for 1 hour, until the pastry is crisp and golden brown.

— · —

Lydney, The Berkeley Viaduct c1955 L200024

The last railway bridge to cross the River Severn before the open sea, the Berkeley Viaduct linked Sharpness and Lydney. It was built as part of the old Great Western Railway between 1875 and 1879, and consisted of two main spans and nineteen lesser spans, with a steam-operated swinging section over the Gloucester to Berkeley Canal. An oil barge struck it in 1960, and two of the spans were brought down. The remainder was subsequently demolished.

Elvers

On dark nights in early spring, the River Severn is lit with hundreds of lights along both banks, each with a fisherman keenly waiting to catch elvers on the first spring tide of the season.... These are elvermen, who annually take their strange-looking nets to the river in the hope of securing a large catch of translucent, worm-like fish. Elvers were a local delicacy for centuries, and were once sold in pint mugs around the city streets of Gloucester before being cooked alive by housewives in a frying pan, together with the fat from a nice piece of bacon. Another local speciality was known as Elver Cakes, which was a form of pie. These little elvers (baby eels) have taken three years to travel from the Sargasso Sea in the North Atlantic to the Severn at Gloucester, and if they are lucky enough to escape being caught, they will then remain here for a number of years before returning home again to breed. They now command high prices around the world, but if you do manage to acquire some, here is a recipe for fried elvers.

> 450g/1 lb fresh elvers
> 15g/1oz seasoned flour
> Oil for deep frying
> 1 lemon

Wash the elvers well with salted water. Coat them with the seasoned flour, making sure that all parts are covered or they will stick together when they are fried. Heat the oil and deep-fry the elvers until they are crisp, then serve with lemon wedges.

Gloucester, Fishing for Elvers 2004 G20701

'A surfeit of lampreys ...'

Rather unattractive eel-like fish which are caught in the Severn are lampreys. These are parasitical, having jawless mouths with a ring of teeth that they use as a powerful sucker to latch on to other fish and feed on their blood, and also hitch a ride up the Severn estuary. They are sometimes called 'nine-eyes' locally, because they have seven gill slits running along their sides, which look like extra eyes.

Lampreys have two poisonous filaments running down their back which must be cut off before cooking. They are seldom eaten nowadays as their flesh is very rich and fatty, but in medieval times they were considered a great delicacy. From the early Middle Ages it was customary for the Corporation of Gloucester to send a lamprey pie to the reigning monarch each Christmas; this tradition lasted up to 1836, although Gloucester still sends a Royal Lamprey Pie to the monarch to mark particularly special occasions – Queen Elizabeth II received one for her coronation day banquet in 1953 and also on the occasion of her Silver Jubilee in 1977.

In the Middle Ages, King John enjoyed lampreys so much that in the year 1200 he fined the city of Gloucester 40 marks for forgetting to send him his lamprey pie, complaining that 'they did not pay sufficient respect in the matter of his lampreys'. King John was obviously not put off enjoying his delicacy by the fact that his great-grandfather, King Henry I, famously died in 1135 after gorging on a 'a surfeit of lampreys'.

Gloucester, The Docks 1950 G20052

RECIPE

— . —

Baked Stuffed Trout

Angling is a popular pastime in the Cotswolds, where there are a number of rivers and lakes where brown and rainbow trout, grayling, chubb, roach, pike and carp can be caught. One of the best Cotswold rivers is the Coln, which rises near Sevenhampton and flows through the Cotswolds before joining the Thames near Lechlade. There are also a number of commercial fisheries, many of which have been developed from former gravel pits, such as those at the Cotswolds Water Park near Cirencester. This recipe serves 4 people, so increase the quantities for more.

> 4 trout, gutted and cleaned, with fins and gills removed
> 115g/4oz fresh breadcrumbs
> 115g/4oz butter
> Grated rind and juice of 1 lemon
> Salt and pepper to taste
> 1 egg yolk
> 25g/1oz plain flour
> 300ml/ ½ pint milk

Pre-heat the oven to 180°C/350°F/Gas Mark 4.

Melt half the butter in a heavy-bottomed pan, and add the breadcrumbs, lemon rind, salt and pepper. Remove from the heat and allow the mixture to cool a little, then beat in the egg yolk to form a firm stuffing. Use the stuffing to fill the cavity of each fish. Place the stuffed fish in a greased, ovenproof dish, dot the top with small knobs of butter, and bake in the pre-heated oven for 30 minutes.

Whilst the fish are cooking, melt the remaining butter in a saucepan, and stir in the flour to make a roux sauce. Cook gently for a few minutes, stirring occasionally, then gradually add the milk, stirring all time, and bring to the boil, still stirring continually, until the sauce has thickened. When the fish are cooked, pour the sauce into the dish with the fish and stir so that it combines with the fish juices. Add the lemon juice, then return the dish to the oven to cook for a further 5 minutes before serving.

— . —

RECIPE

— · —

Trout with Almonds and Cream

This traditional way of serving fresh trout is enough for 4 people, so increase the quantities for more.

> 4 trout, gutted and cleaned
> Flour for coating the fish
> Salt and pepper
> 175g/6oz butter
> 50g/2oz blanched almonds
> Juice of half a lemon
> 150ml/ ¼ pint single cream

Mix the flour with salt and pepper and use to coat the fish on both sides.

Melt 115g/4oz of the butter in a frying pan. Slide in the trout and cook for 15 minutes, turning halfway through cooking time, until they are golden brown on both sides and cooked through. Drain the trout and keep them warm on a serving dish.

Clean the pan, then melt the remaining butter in it. Add the almonds and fry carefully until they are lightly browned. Stir in the lemon juice.

Heat the cream gently in a separate pan and pour over the fish. Sprinkle with the almonds and serve.

— · —

Bourton-on-the-Water, The Model Village c1950 B392051

MEAT

Chipping Norton, The Cotswolds c1960 C288067

The Cotswolds are an upland area of limestone. The escarpment, 'the Cotswold edge', rises above the broad valley of the River Severn, and the land slopes gently away eastward. The main area of the Cotswolds is contained in Gloucestershire, but it extends eastwards into Oxfordshire and to some degree into Worcestershire, Warwickshire, Wiltshire and Somerset. The Cotswold region has been designated as an Area of Outstanding Natural Beauty. The Cotswold Hills have always been famous for sheep rearing, and lamb features in many recipes from this area – indeed, the Old English word 'cots' in the name of the Cotswolds referred to a place where sheep were kept, and 'wolds' meant hills.

RECIPE

—.—

Gloucestershire Squab Pie

Lamb features in many of the recipes from Gloucestershire and the Cotswolds area, such as Gloucestershire Squab Pie. Squab pies would originally have been made with young pigeons (called squabs), but over time it became more usual to make them with lamb and slices of cooking apple, flavoured with spices.

> 675g/1½ lbs lamb neck fillets, cut into 12 pieces
> 1 onion, thinly sliced
> 350g/12oz leeks, sliced
> 1 large cooking apple, peeled, cored and diced
> Half a teaspoonful of allspice
> Half a teaspoonful of freshly grated nutmeg
> 150ml/¼ pint lamb, beef or vegetable stock
> 225g/8oz shortcrust pastry
> Beaten egg or milk to glaze
> Salt and pepper

Pre-heat the oven to 200°C/400°F/Gas Mark 6.

Layer the meat, onion, leek and apple in a pie dish, sprinkling in the spices and seasoning as you go, to taste. Pour in the stock.

Roll out the pastry to 2cm (¾ inch) larger than the top of the pie dish. Cut a narrow strip from around the pastry, fit it around the dampened rim of the dish, then brush with water. Lay the pastry over the dish, and press the edges together to seal them. Brush the pastry lid with beaten egg or milk, and make a hole in the centre.

Bake the pie in the pre-heated oven for 20 minutes, then reduce the oven temperature to 180°C/350°F/Gas Mark 4 and continue to cook for 1-1¼ hours, covering the pie with foil if the pastry starts to brown too much.

—.—

Stow-on-the-Wold
The Square and St Edward's Hall
c1950 S260014

'Stow-on-the-Wold, where the wind blows cold' warns an old local adage. Sitting on the Roman Fosse Way, 800 feet up on a rounded tump, the surrounding countryside was excellent sheep country in the past. Wool merchants thrived and built themselves fine houses in Stow. The heart of Stow is its Square, where stalls were first set up for the Thursday market (which continues to this day) in 1107. Local lore says that the buildings were clustered so tightly around the Square at Stow-on-the-Wold to keep the wind off the farmers on market days. Daniel Defoe visited the town in the early 18th century and recorded that 20,000 sheep were sold at Stow-on-the-Wold market in the year prior to his visit. Squeezed between the buildings in Stow's Square are alleys, known locally as 'tures' (an abbreviation of 'aperture'). On market days in time gone by, sheep were driven in single file along these narrow ways to be counted.

RECIPE

—·—

Lamb Chops Portmanteau'd

This dish was named after a small travelling bag known as a 'portmanteau' which the lamb chops resemble when they have been stuffed with their filling and cooked. The Cotswolds were prime fox-hunting territory in the past, and this used to be a popular dish to serve to gentlemen at hunt breakfasts. Thick lamb chops need to be chosen to make this. Serves 4.

> 4 thick loin lamb chops, trimmed of fat
> 50g/2oz butter
> 8 chicken livers, trimmed and chopped into small pieces
> 8 mushrooms, finely chopped
> 1 egg, beaten
> 50g/2oz dried breadcrumbs, seasoned with salt and pepper

Pre-heat the oven to 200°C/400°F/Gas Mark 6.

Use a very sharp knife to cut a horizontal slit right up to the bone in each chop, to make a pocket large enough to be stuffed.

Melt half the butter in a frying pan, add the chicken livers and mushrooms and fry gently for 4-5 minutes, until soft but not browned. Leave to cool for a few minutes, then use the mixture to stuff the pockets in the lamb chops. Sew up the pockets with trussing thread.

Dip each chop first in the beaten egg and then into the seasoned breadcrumbs, pressing the breadcrumbs on with your fingers, to make sure that the chops are coated thoroughly. Place the chops in a baking dish. Melt the remaining butter and pour it over the chops. Bake in the pre-heated oven for 7-10 minutes, depending on how 'pink' you like your lamb, then turn the chops over and bake for a further 7-10 minutes, until the chops are golden brown on both sides. Serve at once, whilst the chops are piping hot and crispy.

—·—

RECIPE

—·—

Stuffed Skirt of Beef

This is a very old Gloucestershire recipe for an economical and nourishing way of cooking one of the cheaper cuts of beef.

1kg/2 lbs skirt of beef
50g/2oz dripping (or oil, for browning the meat)
225g/8oz onion, finely chopped
1.2 litres/2 pints beef stock
Salt and pepper
115g/4oz carrots, sliced
115g/4oz turnip, peeled and chopped into small chunks
50g/2oz cornflour
2 tablespoonfuls of water

For the stuffing:
115g/4oz medium oatmeal
50g/2oz shredded suet
1 tablespoonful of chopped fresh parsley and other herbs of choice
25g/1oz onion, very finely chopped
A little milk

Buy the skirt of beef in one piece. Remove the skin and slice a deep pocket in the meat with a sharp knife. Combine all the stuffing ingredients together, using just enough milk to bind it to a stiff consistency. Fill the pocket in the meat with the stuffing and sew up the opening with trussing thread. Melt the dripping (or oil) in a large, heavy saucepan and brown the meat and the onions. Add the stock, and season to taste, if necessary. Bring to the boil, then reduce heat, cover the pan and simmer very gently for 2½ - 3 hours, until the meat is tender. About 45 minutes before the end of the cooking time, add the carrots and turnip to the pan. When the meat is ready to serve, blend the cornflour with the water, and add it to the pan to thicken the gravy. Lift out the meat and remove the trussing thread, and serve it on a hot dish surrounded by the carrots and turnips, and serve the gravy separately.

—·—

Cirencester, Oxen Team in Cirencester Park 1898 40986

Although working bullocks were used on Cotswold farms until well into the 19th century, particularly for compressing steambeds and millponds, those used on Lord Bathurst's estate at Cirencester Park for ploughing were regarded as something of an anachronism, even though these huge beasts consumed less than horses and possessed greater stamina.

RECIPE

Gloucestershire Cottage Pie

This is a good way of using leftover beef and gravy. It was traditionally served cold, with salad.

450g/1 lb cooked beef
115g/4oz cooked bacon or ham
225g/8oz cold potatoes
115g/4oz fresh breadcrumbs
25g/1oz butter or margarine
1 egg
2 onions, peeled and chopped
Salt and pepper
Leftover gravy

Mince the cold beef and bacon together, and season well. Fry the chopped onions in the butter or margarine until soft and starting to brown, then add enough gravy to cover and boil for 10 minutes. Mix together the egg, meat, bacon, potatoes and breadcrumbs, then add this to the gravy mixture and combine it all well together. Turn the mixture into a greased pie dish, or a loaf tin lined with foil, and bake for 30 minutes in a pre-heated oven at 180°C/350°F/Gas Mark 4.

Bibury, Arlington Row c1960 B530002

RECIPE

—·—

Gammon and Apricots

This was a traditional dish to serve at the harvest suppers that used to be held on farms to celebrate the harvest being safely gathered in. This time of the year was also when apricots became ripe and ready to eat.

    450g/1 lb gammon rasher
    25g/1oz butter
    350g/12oz fresh apricots (or dried apricots,
      soaked in water overnight)
    25g/1oz sultanas
    Pepper
    300ml/ ½ pint stock
    675g/1½ potatoes

Pre-heat the oven to 180°C/350°F/Gas Mark 4.

Melt the butter in a frying pan and fry the gammon rasher lightly on both sides, then put the gammon into a casserole dish.

Stone and coarsely chop the apricots, then put the apricots and sultanas on top of the gammon rasher, and season to taste with pepper. Pour over the stock.

Peel the potatoes, cut them into thin slices and arrange them on top of the gammon and apricots. Cover the casserole dish with its lid, and bake in the pre-heated oven for 1 hour.

—·—

Stroud, King Street 1910 62677

Gloucestershire Old Spots Pigs

The Gloucestershire Old Spots breed of pig, characterised by large black spots on its skin, was developed to thrive on the whey that was a by-product of Gloucestershire's cheese industry, and, particularly, windfall apples in the county's orchards – it is often referred to as 'The Orchard Pig'. The meat is well-flavoured and makes excellent Gloucester (or Gloster) Sausages, but above all this is the pork to seek out at good butchers and farmers' markets if you want to serve up a great joint of roast pork with wonderful crispy, puffy crackling. Do not be put off by a good layer of fat on the joint, as this is where much of the flavour is. To ensure really good crackling, pat the skin of the joint dry with kitchen paper before cooking, then score the skin of the joint with a very sharp knife (a Stanley knife is ideal), making a number of deep, parallel cuts at regular intervals. Then rub all over the skin with plenty of salt, making sure that you also rub it well into the slash lines (a mixture of sea salt and regular kitchen salt is best), put the joint into a shallow roasting dish, and do not add any oil or fat – plastering extra fat on the joint is the death of good crackling!

A boned loin joint of around 1.5kg (about 3½ lbs) of good quality pork with a good layer of fatty skin will give you a succulent roast with excellent crackling, and is a handy size for four or five people. Prepare the joint as above, then put it into a pre-heated oven at 245°C/475°F/Gas Mark 9. Roast for 25 minutes, then reduce the heat to 190°C/375°F/Gas Mark 5 and roast for a further one hour. You won't need to baste the joint during cooking as the fat in the meat will keep it moist. If the crackling is not quite hard and crisp at the end of the cooking time, turn up the heat to 220°C/425°F/Gas Mark 7 and cook for a further 10-15 minutes. Remove the meat from the oven, cover with foil and allow to 'rest' for 15-20 minutes before carving the pork into slices, and serve with strips of crackling, apple sauce, vegetables, gravy and roast, boiled or mashed potatoes.

RECIPE

— · —

Pork with Apples and Cider Sauce

Think of Gloucestershire and cider, and Laurie Lee's famous book 'Cider With Rosie' comes to mind (see page 83). Use Gloucestershire cider to make a delicious creamy sauce to accompany pork in this recipe.

25g/1oz butter
500g/1¼ lbs pork fillet or tenderloin, cut into small pieces
12 baby onions or shallots, peeled and left whole
2 teaspoonfuls grated lemon rind
300ml/ ½ pint dry Gloucestershire cider
150ml/ ¼ pint stock
2 crisp eating apples, cored and sliced but not peeled
3 tablespoonfuls chopped fresh parsley
100ml/3½ fl oz whipping cream
Salt and pepper

Heat the butter in a large sauté or frying pan, and brown the pork in batches. Transfer the pork to a bowl. Add the onions to the pan and cook gently until they are soft. Stir in the lemon rind, cider and stock, increase heat and boil for a few minutes. Return the pork to the pan, reduce heat and cook gently for 25-30 minutes, until the meat is tender. Add the apples to the pan and cook for a further 5 minutes.

Use a slotted spoon to transfer the pork, apples and onions to a warmed serving dish, and keep warm. Stir the cream and parsley into the cooking pan, and allow the sauce to bubble so that it thickens slightly. Season to taste, then pour over the pork and serve whilst it is hot.

— · —

Tewkesbury, Church Street 1907 59072

RECITE

—.—

Sirloin Steaks with Tewkesbury Mustard

In past centuries, the town of Tewkesbury gave its name to a method of making a particularly thick, fiery mustard which included horseradish in its ingredients. It was originally made, transported and sold in the form of small balls of mustard mixture which had been dried to aid preservation. The mustard balls would be broken apart when they were needed for use and then mixed to a creamy consistency with liquid (which could be water, wine, ale or cider). The mustard was mentioned by Shakespeare in 'Henry IV, Part 2', when Sir John Falstaff says 'His wit's as thick as Tewkesbury mustard'. The mustard also gave rise to a phrase used in Gloucestershire to describe someone whose expression is sad, severe or stern: 'He looks as if he lived on Tewkesbury mustard'. The making of Tewkesbury mustard was revived in the late 20th century. Several manufacturers now produce it commercially, and the Waitrose supermarket chain sells its own-label version. Because Tewkesbury mustard is made with finely-grated horseradish as well as mustard seeds, it goes particularly well with beef. This recipe is for four people – increase the quantities for more.

    4 sirloin steaks
    50g/2oz Tewkesbury mustard
    15g/ ½ oz plain flour
    2 tablespoonfuls chopped fresh parsley
    2 tablespoonfuls chopped fresh thyme

Pre-heat the grill. Mix together the mustard and the flour, and spread the mixture on top of the sirloin steaks. Line the grill pan with tin foil and sprinkle the foil with the chopped fresh herbs. Place the steaks on the foil, on top of the herbs, and grill for 5-15 minutes (depending on how you like your steak cooked), turning the steaks frequently until they are cooked to taste.

—.—

'Rook Pie, anyone?'

Rook Pie was often eaten by country people in the past, sometimes served with the feet of the rooks sticking out of the centre of the crust, although a more usual way was to take just the breast and upper legs of the bird for the pie. Only the younger birds were used, so Rook Pie was usually eaten in spring and early summer. Other traditional dishes which were often eaten in this area in the past, and which are very much not to modern tastes, were Lambs' Tail Pie, made from the docked tails of lambs, and Muggety Pie, made from the umbilical cords of new-born calves.

Birdlip, Village Life 1907 59061x

CHEESE AND VEGETABLE DISHES

Gloucestershire is famous for its Double Gloucester cheese, with its characteristic orange colour achieved by the addition of annatto, a natural colouring. In former times, the milk of different breeds of cow was used to make different cheeses, and traditionally the Old Gloucester breed was considered the only cow for making Double Gloucester cheese – the milk from this breed had very small fat globules, which gave the cheese a special fine texture. Gloucester cheese used to be made in two varieties, Single Gloucester and Double Gloucester, but only Double Gloucester is made nowadays. Traditionally, Double Gloucester was produced on farms using mainly the morning's milk, with just a little from the evening's milking, and was made in large cheeses weighing between 15 and 25 pounds that took several months to mature. Single Gloucester was made from either the morning's milk or skimmed evening milk and much smaller cheeses were made, weighing between nine and twelve pounds – this did not need ripening, and was mainly eaten on the farms where it was made, rather than sold. In the past, barge-loads of Double Gloucester cheese used to be carried up the Thames from Lechlade to London. Although the Round House at Lechlade looks like a Gothic folly, this round house was lived in by a 'lengthman' and his family, who collected the tolls from passing barges on the Thames and Severn canal. Built in the latter half of the 18th century, this man-made waterway stretched from Inglesham to Stroud, where it joined the Stroudwater Navigation leading to the River Severn at Framilode.

Lechlade
The Round House
c1960 L147026

RECITE

~ . ~

Gloucester Cheese Stew

This tasty cheese and potato bake makes an ideal supper dish.

450g/1 lb potatoes
275ml/ ½ pint milk
Salt and freshly ground black pepper
3 onions
225g/8oz Double Gloucester cheese, grated

Peel the potatoes, cut them into thin slices and place in a saucepan with the milk. Season with salt and pepper, then simmer them gently until almost tender (10-15 minutes). Take the potato slices out of the pan, and reserve the milk. Peel the onions and chop them finely. Grease a medium-sized casserole or ovenproof dish. Put layers of potato, onion and cheese into the dish, seasoning each layer, finishing with a layer of cheese. Pour over the milk that the potatoes were cooked in. Bake the dish, uncovered, for one hour in a medium oven – 180°C/350°F/Gas Mark 4 – until the top is golden brown.

Gloucester, Hare Lane, First Sunday School 1892
29907

~ . ~

Cheese Rolling

Coopers Hill near Brockworth is where – depending on the current Health & Safety legislation – the famous cheese-rolling event traditionally takes place on Whit Monday in May (now the Spring Bank Holiday Monday). This continues a bizarre, centuries-old tradition, in which participants race down a precipitous slope in pursuit of a Double Gloucester cheese – the first person over the finishing line at the bottom of the hill wins the cheese. It began as an event just for people from Brockworth but now attracts people from over the world who wish to take part in this eccentric English occasion.

Brockworth, Coopers Hill 1907 59070

RECIPE

~ . ~

Gloucestershire Cheese and Ale

The regional version of toasted cheese is Gloucestershire Cheese and Ale.

225g/8oz Double Gloucester cheese
1 teaspoonful of made mustard
300ml/ ½ pint brown ale
8 thick slices of wholemeal bread

Pre-heat the oven to 230°C/450°F/Gas Mark 8. Grate the cheese and place it in an ovenproof dish. Spread the surface of the cheese with mustard, and pour on the ale. Bake in the pre-heated oven until the cheese has melted – about 5-10 minutes. Whilst the cheese is melting, toast the bread slices. Place the pieces of toast in individual wide serving bowls, and when the cheese and ale mixture is ready, pour some over each piece of toast and serve immediately, whilst it is piping hot.

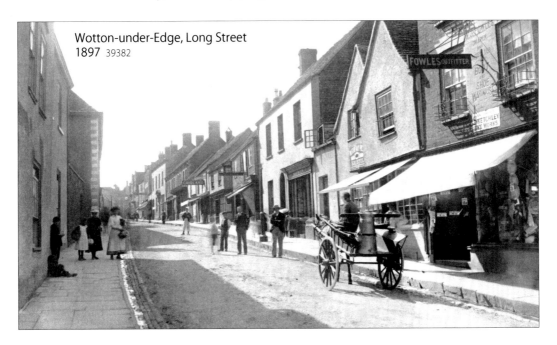

Wotton-under-Edge, Long Street
1897 39382

~ . ~

RECURSIVE

—·—

Cotswold Cheese Dumplings

These traditional savoury dumplings can be served hot with vegetables or a tomato sauce, or cold with a salad or as snacks with drinks. They can be made with any hard cheese of choice, but in this recipe the cheese marketed as 'Cotswold cheese' is used – a Double Gloucester cheese with the addition of chives and onions.

    50g/2oz Cotswold cheese
    25g/1oz butter or margarine
    1 egg, beaten
    Salt and pepper
    50g/2oz fresh breadcrumbs
    25g/1oz dried breadcrumbs
    Fat or oil for frying

Grate the cheese finely. Beat the butter or margarine until it is creamy. Mix the grated cheese and creamed fat together, then add the beaten egg, and salt and pepper to taste. Combine the mixture with enough of the fresh breadcrumbs to form a stiff dough.

Turn the dough out onto a lightly floured board, and form it into small balls, or dumplings. Roll the dumplings in the dried breadcrumbs to coat them, then fry them in hot fat until golden brown.

—·—

RECIPE

—.—

Gloucestershire Potato Cakes

These savoury potato cakes made with Double Gloucester cheese make a good snack or supper dish, and are also an unusual way of serving potatoes as a vegetable accompaniment to a meal.

> 450g/1 lb potatoes
> 25g/1oz butter or margarine
> 115g/4oz plain flour
> 115g/4oz Double Gloucester cheese, grated
> 2 eggs, beaten
> Salt and pepper
> Fat or oil for frying

Cook the potatoes in boiling salted water for 10-15 minutes until they are tender. Drain the potatoes then mash them with the butter or margarine. Add the flour and cheese and mix everything together thoroughly. Add the beaten eggs, season to taste with salt and pepper, and combine the mixture well.

Flour your hands and form the mixture into about 8 small cakes, and flatten them slightly. Heat the fat or oil in a frying pan and fry the potato cakes for a few minutes on both sides until they are golden brown.

Alternatively, the potato cakes can be cooked on a greased baking tray in the oven, for about 15 minutes at 200°C/400°F/Gas Mark 6.

—.—

RECISE

—.—

Savoury Carrot Pudding

This recipe for a savoury steamed pudding comes from Dursley, which was once a wool and cloth manufacturing town of some importance. Dursley's quaint yellow Market House was erected in 1738 and stands on 13 arches. The upper storey was used as a town hall, whilst market business was conducted on the open arcade of the ground floor – at one time, the local cheese and butter market was held there. Local people were so grateful to Queen Anne for money given to repair the parish church tower after part of it fell down in 1699 that they placed a statue of her in the upper niche of the Market House.

225g/8oz grated carrots
450g/1 lb cooked and mashed potatoes
225g/8oz sausage meat
Salt and pepper
A pinch of grated nutmeg
1 teaspoonful chopped fresh parsley
1 onion, finely chopped
1 egg, beaten
A little milk or stock, for mixing

Mix together the carrots, potatoes and sausage meat with the seasoning, nutmeg, parsley, onion and beaten egg, adding a little milk or stock if necessary if the mixture seems to dry. Place the mixture in a greased 1.2 litre (2 pint) pudding basin, and cover with pleated greaseproof paper (to allow room for rising during cooking) and foil, and tie down firmly.

Place the pudding basin in a large saucepan of boiling water and cover the pan with its lid. Steam for about 2 hours, topping up the pan with more boiling water when necessary, and ensuring that the pan does not boil dry. Serve with brown gravy.

—.—

Dursley, Market House c1947 D72028

Dialect Words from Gloucestershire and the Cotswolds

'**Above a bit**' – a good amount, more than enough.

'**Adry**' – thirsty.

'**Afeard**' – afraid.

'**Afterclaps**' – consequences.

'**A-ground**' – on foot.

'**A-hopping**' – fretting, worrying.

'**Airsens**' – haws, the berries of the hawthorn tree.

'**Artishrew**' – the harvest mouse.

'**Asker**' – a newt.

'**Backrackets**' – fireworks.

'**Badger**' – a dealer in commodities in olden times, ie a butter dealer was known as a 'butter badger'.

'**Bandy**' – a tool for spreading dung in fields, thus the phrase 'to bandy about' – throw something around indiscriminately.

'**Candle of the eye**' – the pupil of the eye.

'**Candlemas bells**' – snowdrops. (The old Christian festival of Candlemas is 2nd February, when snowdrops are in flower.)

'**Chackle**' – a clattering or rattling noise.

'**Cherry curds**' – the first milk produced by a cow after calving.

'**Chesle money**' – the name given by Gloucestershire people to the Roman coins they often found in the ground.

'**Chubby**' – the hedge-sparrow.

'**Chur**' or '**chore**' – a small alley between houses.

'**Clack**' – noise.

'**Dabbly**' – wet, rainy.

'**Darricky**' – rotten (as of wood).

'**Dew-bit**' – the first food eaten in the morning.

'**Dilling pig**' or '**dolly pig**' – the runt, the weakest piglet of a litter.

'**Emmet**' an ant, thus '**Emmet tump**' – an anthill.

'**Flummock**' – a slovenly, untidy person.

'**Gammut**' – a joke, or mischievous behaviour.

'**Happen**' – perhaps.

'**Joggetting**' – shaking.

'**Ladycow**' – ladybird.

'**Lagged**' – wearied, tired.

'**Maggot**' – a magpie.

'**Mugglement**' – a state of muddle and confusion.

'**Nesh**' – tender, weak, delicate.

'**Nettlesome**' – quarrelsome.

'**Peep**' – dawn, ie 'It had just peeped' – dawn had just broken.

'**Putchen**' – an eel basket.

'**Rangled**' – tangled.

'**Robin Redbreast's pincushion**' – the red hairy gall on the wild rose.

'**Scratcher**' – a roller with iron teeth used for breaking up apples for cider-making.

'**Screech-drossle**' – the missel thrush.

'**Tarry**' – to wait.

'**Tiddlin**' – a lamb brought up by hand.

'**Tump**' – a mound or a hummock.

'**Watty-handed**' – left-handed.

'**Whinnock**' – to whimper.

'**Wozzled**' – trampled down.

Cheltenham, High Street 1901 47265

PUDDINGS AND DESSERTS

Just inside Worcestershire is the Cotswold village of Broadway, sometimes described as the prettiest village in England, with its handsome houses in honey-hued stone and a village green shaded by chestnut trees. Now the major tourist centre of the north Cotswolds, back in the 17th century Broadway was a thriving staging post and horse-drawn carriages by the dozen stopped to feed and water en route to London from Worcester. At that time, over 30 inns in the village offered passengers refreshment and accommodation. This lucrative trade came to an end with the arrival of the railway, and the end of stagecoaches, but the railways enabled the surrounding countryside to be developed into one of the country's most important market gardening areas, sited as it is on the edge of the fertile Vale of Evesham.

Broadway, The Village 1899 44113

RECIPE

— . —

Plum and Walnut Crumble

From the great resources of the nearby Vale of Evesham and Severn Valley, fruit has always been easily available in the area, particularly apples, damsons and plums. Gloucestershire was also noted in the past for its walnuts, especially around Arlingham, near Stroud. In 1807 Thomas Rudge commented on the walnut trees there in his 'General View of the Agriculture of Gloucestershire': 'In the parish of Arlingham there are more, perhaps, than in many other parishes combined; so abundant, indeed, is the fruit this year (1805) that it is become an article of commerce, and two vessels are now being laded with walnuts for Scotland . . . the produce of a tree is highly valuable, as 20,000 are not considered an extravagant calculation for a large tree.'

75g/3oz walnut pieces
75g/3oz butter or margarine, diced
175g/6oz plain flour
175g/6oz demerara sugar
1kg/2 lbs plums, halved and stoned

Pre-heat the oven to 180°C/350°F/Gas Mark 4.

Spread the nuts on a baking sheet and place in the oven for 8-10 minutes, until they are evenly coloured.

Grease a 1.2 litre (2 pint) ovenproof dish. Put the plums into the dish and stir in the nuts and half the demerara sugar. Rub the butter or margarine into the flour until the mixture resembles coarse breadcrumbs. Stir in the remaining sugar and continue to rub in until fine crumbs are formed. Cover the fruit with the crumb mixture and press it down lightly. Bake the pudding in the pre-heated oven for about 45 minutes, until the top is golden brown and the fruit tender. Serve with custard or cream.

— . —

RECIPE

—·—

Crundle Pudding

This recipe comes from the village of Weston Subedge, near Chipping Campden.

50g/2oz plain flour
50g/2oz butter
50g/2oz caster sugar
1 egg, separated
300ml/ ½ pint milk

Pre-heat the oven to 180°C/350°F/Gas Mark 4.

Grease an ovenproof pie dish. Cream the butter and sugar together until light and fluffy, then mix in the flour. Beat the white of the egg until it is stiff then add the egg yolk to it and beat again. Add the egg to the mixture then, just before putting the pudding in the oven, add the milk, stirring it in gradually – this must only be done at the very last moment.

Turn the mixture into the prepared pie dish and bake in the pre-heated oven for about 30 minutes.

This was traditionally served with warmed black treacle and cream.

—·—

Chipping Campden, Church Street and the Almshouses c1935 C335005

Chipping Campden, Leasebourne c1950 C335034

Winchcombe, Gloucester Street 1907 59459

RECIPE

—·—

Syllabub

Sudeley Castle near Winchcombe was the final home of Henry VIII's last – and surviving – wife, Queen Catherine Parr. After King Henry's death she married Thomas Seymour and lived at Sudeley Castle with him and her step-daughter, Princess (later Queen) Elizabeth. Queen Catherine died in childbirth at Sudeley in 1548, and her marble tomb stands in St Mary's Church in the castle grounds. The Sudeley Castle that Queen Catherine knew was ruined during the Civil War, but was restored and rebuilt in the 19th century. Syllabub was a popular dessert in Tudor times, and is just the sort of dish that would have been enjoyed by Queen Catherine and Princess Elizabeth at Sudeley Castle.

150ml/ ¼ pint white wine
2 tablespoonfuls lemon juice
2 teaspoonfuls lemon zest
75g/3oz caster sugar
300ml/ ½ pint double cream

Put the wine, lemon juice, zest and sugar into a bowl. Leave to stand for at least three hours. Add the cream and whip until the mixture stands in soft peaks. Transfer to 6 wine glasses or glass dishes and decorate with lemon zest. Chill for several hours before serving.

Sudeley Castle c1960 S745010

—·—

Minchinhampton, The Market House 1901 47348

The attractive market town of Minchinhampton is situated on a hilltop spur of
the western escarpment of the Cotstwolds between Nailsworth and Stroud.
Minchinhampton's fine Market Hall dates from 1698, and demonstrates the
early prosperity of this important wool town. It was built to house the local wool
market by Philip Sheppard, whose ancestor Samuel had bought the manor of
Minchinhampton in 1651. It is supported on an arcade of pillars that are unusual
in that they are made of stone on the outside, and timber on the inside. Market
houses of this design are found throughout the Cotswolds. The upper storey
often served as the town hall, while market traders set up their stalls on the open-
sided ground floor.

RECIPE

—·—

Potato Pudding

The potato was often used in the past as an ingredient in sweet puddings or pies, which were eaten as dessert dishes. This is an old Gloucestershire recipe for a sweet pudding made with potatoes.

> 225g/8oz floury potatoes, peeled
> 2 eggs, beaten
> 50g/2oz caster sugar
> 1 lemon
> 50g/2oz butter
> 50g/2oz sultanas

Pre-heat the oven to 180°C/350°F/Gas Mark 4. Grease an ovenproof pie dish.

Cook the potatoes in boiling salted water for about 20 minutes, or until they are soft and tender. Drain the potatoes, then mash them well or pass them through a sieve or blender, and mix with the butter, sugar, lemon juice and grated lemon rind, sultanas and beaten eggs. Combine it all together so that it is well mixed, then pour the mixture into the greased pie dish.

Bake in the pre-heated oven for about 40 minutes, until the pudding is firm to the touch and lightly browned. Serve hot, with cream or custard.

—·—

RECIPE

—.—

Heg Peg Dump

St Margaret, the patron saint of safe childbirth, was a popular saint in the Middle Ages. Her feast day on 20th July was particularly remembered in Gloucestershire, when a special pudding known as Heg Peg Dump was made. This was traditionally a suetcrust dumpling containing wild fruit such as plums or damsons, hence the strange name: Heg for hedgerow, Peg for Margaret, and Dump for dumpling.

For the suetcrust pastry:
225g/8oz self-raising flour
Half a teaspoonful salt
1 teaspoonful baking powder
115g/4oz shredded suet
150ml/ ¼ pint cold water

For the filling:
450g/1 lb plums or damsons, stoned
225g/8oz cooking apples, peeled,
 cored and cut into slices
175g/6oz sugar
1 tablespoonful water

Sift the flour, salt and baking powder into a bowl. Add the suet and mix together lightly, adding enough water to mix to a soft dough. Turn out the dough onto a lightly floured surface and knead the dough until it is smooth and pliable. Save a third of the dough to make a lid and roll out the rest thinly.

Use the rolled out pastry to line a greased 1.2 litre (2 pint) pudding basin. Fill the pastry-lined pudding basin with alternate layers of the fruit and sugar. Pour in the tablespoonful of water. Moisten the edges of the pudding pastry with water, and cover with a lid rolled out from the reserved pastry. Press the edges firmly together to seal them.

Cover the pudding basin with a lid made of pleated greaseproof paper and then another of foil, and tie down securely with string. Place the pudding basin in a large pan of boiling water, cover the pan with its lid and steam over boiling water for 2½ - 3 hours, replenishing the pan with more boiling water when necessary, and ensuring that the pan does not boil dry. When the pudding is cooked, serve from the basin with custard or cream.

—.—

Stroud, High Street 1910 62676

A Taste of GLOUCESTERSHIRE & THE COTSWOLDS

Coleford, The Speech House 1893 32450

The Forest of Dean area of Gloucestershire was a royal hunting preserve in ancient times and is a place with a wealth of history and a sense of independence that is tangible in its ancient customs, lore and laws. As well as forestry and charcoal production, coal mining and iron working were at the heart of the Forest's economy until these industries went into decline on a commercial scale in the 1960s. Even today, though, Freeminers exercise their rights to dig coal, iron ore and ochre from private pits, as they have done for generations beyond recall. Despite its industrial heritage, the Forest of Dean remains an area of mixed woodland roamed by wild deer and common land used for pasturing livestock. One of the most famous buildings in the Forest is what is now the Speech House Hotel, between Cinderford and Coleford. The Speech House was originally built in the 17th century as the Verderers' and Foresters' Court, where disputes between miners and foresters were heard and settled and where the Forest Law Courts were held. Although the Verderers' Court of the Speech House is now used as the hotel's magnificent oak-beamed restaurant, adorned with 19 pairs of antlers, it still continues in its original function as the courtroom and meeting place of the Foresters of Dean, who are concerned with administrating Forest Law and managing and protecting the 'vert and venison' of the Forest – the local deer and their habitat. The pudding on the opposite page was a traditional speciality served at the Speech House in the past.

64

RECIPE

—·—

Speech House Pudding

115g/4oz butter, softened to room temperature
50g/2oz caster sugar
4 eggs, separated
115g/4oz plain flour
2 large tablespoonfuls raspberry jam
1 teaspoonful bicarbonate of soda
2 tablespoonfuls milk
Extra raspberry jam to make a sauce

Grease a 1.2 litre (2 pint) pudding basin with a little of the butter. In another basin, cream together the butter and sugar until light and fluffy. Beat in the beaten egg yolks, a little at a time, alternating with a spoonful of the flour, beating well after each addition. Beat in any remaining flour. Mix in the two tablespoonfuls of jam and combine well.

In a separate bowl, whisk the egg whites until they are stiff and stand in peaks.

Mix the bicarbonate of soda into the milk and stir it into the flour mixture. Use a large metal spoon to quickly fold the beaten egg whites into the mixture, very gently but thoroughly. Pour the mixture into the prepared pudding basin (it should only be about three-quarters full). Cover the basin with its lid, or make a lid out of a piece of pleated greaseproof paper and then another piece of kitchen foil (to allow room for expansion during cooking), and tie it down securely with kitchen string. Place the pudding basin in a large pan of boiling water, cover the pan with its lid and steam over boiling water for 2½ - 3 hours, replenishing the pan with more boiling water when necessary, to ensure that the pan does not boil dry. When the pudding is cooked, turn it out by inverting the basin over a large warmed plate and tipping it out. Heat up more raspberry jam to make a sauce and serve the pudding with the jam sauce poured over the top, and also a little cream if required.

—·—

RECITE

— . —

Apple Cobs

Apple Cobs is the Gloucestershire name for Apple Dumplings, which can be made with either shortcrust or suetcrust pastry.

> 4 large cooking apples
> 50g/2oz soft brown sugar
> 25g/1oz butter
> Half a teaspoonful ground cinnamon
> Grated rind of 1 lemon
> 225g/8oz shortcrust or suetcrust pastry, as preferred
> Milk to glaze
> Caster sugar

Pre-heat the oven to 180°C/350°F/Gas Mark 4.

Peel and core the apples.

Divide the pastry into four equal pieces. Roll each piece out into a square big enough to wrap around an apple. Place one apple in the centre of each square. Mix the sugar, lemon peel and cinnamon together and use the mixture to fill the cavity of each apple, and place a knob of butter on top of the mixture.

Dampen the edges of each piece of pastry with water, and fold up the corners to meet at the top like a parcel, and enclose each apple. Pinch the pastry edges well together to seal.

Place the dumplings – join downwards – in a greased ovenproof dish and brush with milk to glaze. Bake in the pre-heated oven for about half an hour – test by sticking a skewer into the dumpling to make sure the apple is soft. Sprinkle with caster sugar, and serve with custard or cream.

— . —

RECIPE

—·—

Cheltenham Pudding

175g/6oz plain flour
1 teaspoonful baking powder
Half a teaspoonful grated nutmeg
A pinch of salt
175g/6oz shredded suet
75g/3oz caster sugar
75g/3oz fresh breadcrumbs
50g/2oz raisins
50g/2oz currants
Grated rind of half a lemon
2 eggs, beaten
150ml/ ¼ pint milk

Pre-heat the oven to 190°C/375°F/Gas Mark 5.

Sift the flour, baking powder, nutmeg and salt together into a mixing bowl. Mix in the suet, sugar, breadcrumbs, dried fruit and lemon rind. Stir in the beaten eggs and milk. Beat the mixture well to make a stiff, smooth batter.

Pour the batter into a greased ovenproof dish and bake in the pre-heated oven for 1½ hours.

When cooked, turn out and serve with either a sweet sauce, custard or cream.

—·—

Cheltenham, The Promenade 1923 73481

TEATIME AND BAKING

Bisley, The Seven Springs 1910 62696

Rural, rustic and pretty are the Seven Springs at Bisley. Five of the seven water chutes have gabled canopies, and were restored in 1863 for the Reverend Thomas Keble. Dressing and blessing the springs on Ascension Day is a colourful village affair: the schoolchildren process through the street carrying garlands, and the wells are decorated with spring flowers.

RECIPE

—·—

Blakeney Fritters

This recipe comes from the Gloucestershire village of Blakeney, on the eastern edge of the Forest of Dean. Although these delicacies are called fritters, they are actually more like biscuits.

> 75g/3oz plain flour
> 50g/2oz butter or margarine
> 25g/1oz caster sugar
> 1 egg, separated
> Jam of choice

Put the flour in a bowl and rub in the butter or margarine. Add the sugar and egg yolk, and work the mixture to a paste. Roll little balls of the mixture in your hands and put them on to a lightly-greased baking sheet. Make a hole in each ball with the end of a wooden spoon, and brush them over with a little egg white.

Bake in the pre-heated oven for 30 minutes, until they are just turning golden brown. Put the balls on to a wire rack to cool, then fill the hole in each biscuit with jam.

—·—

RECIPE

—.—

Oldbury Tarts

These small gooseberry tarts (more accurately pies) are named after Oldbury-on-Severn, a village south of Berkeley, where they were often made for Whitsuntide. When you make them, make sure that the edges are well sealed or the sugar will leak out and burn. Oldbury Tarts should be eaten by hand, and are full of juice which runs out when they are bitten into. There is a tradition that there should be 21 points in the crimping that forms a decorative edge around the top of each tart.

> 450g/1 lb plain flour
> 115g/4oz lard
> 115g/4oz butter
> 140ml/5 fl oz boiling water
> 700g/1½ lbs gooseberries, washed, topped and tailed
> 4 dessertspoonfuls demerara sugar
> 1 egg, beaten, to glaze

Sieve the flour into a bowl and make a well in the centre. Cut the lard and the butter into pieces and put into the well in the flour. Pour the boiling water over the fat and stir until it melts, mixing in the flour to make a soft paste. Thinly roll out two-thirds of the pastry on a lightly-floured surface and cut it into 15 cm (6 inch) rounds. Hand-raise the edges of each pastry round by pleating the sides 4 or 5 times and bringing them up to form a pie shell. Put the prepared gooseberries together with one dessertspoon of brown sugar into the centre of each shell. From the remaining third of pastry, cut an equal number of smaller circles. Cover each pie shell with a lid made from one of the smaller rounds, moisten the edges, and pinch them together very well all round the tart, to seal the edges and form a decorative rim. Use a sharp knife to cut a small hole in the top of each lid to allow steam to escape during cooking. Transfer the tarts to greased baking sheets and chill in the fridge for 2-3 hours to allow the pastry to firm up.

When ready to cook, pre-heat the oven to 230°C/450°F/Gas Mark 8. Brush each tart with a little beaten egg to glaze, then bake in the pre-heated oven for 10 minutes, then reduce the oven temperature to 180°C/350°F/Gas Mark 4 and bake for a further 20 minutes.

—.—

Berkeley, A Shop 1904 51752v

RECIPE

— . —

Gloucester Tarts

This amount should make about 16 tarts.

> 175g/6oz shortcrust pastry
> 50g/2oz butter or margarine
> 50g/2oz caster sugar
> 1 egg
> 1 teaspoonful almond essence
> 50g/2oz ground rice
> Raspberry or apricot jam
> A little icing sugar, to finish

Pre-heat the oven to 180°C/350°F/Gas Mark 4.

Grease and lightly flour 16 patty tins. Roll out the pastry on a lightly-floured surface and cut it into rounds about 5cm (2 inch) in diameter, and use the rounds to line the patty tins.

Cream the sugar and butter or margarine together until it is light and fluffy. Beat the egg and carefully add it to the creamed mixture, a little at a time, and then stir in the almond essence. Use a large metal spoon to fold in the ground rice and combine the mixture thoroughly together.

Put a spoonful of jam into the bottom of each pastry-lined patty tin, and then cover with a good spoonful of the ground rice mixture. Bake the tarts in the pre-heated oven for about 15-20 minutes, until the filling is lightly golden and firm to the touch. Leave to cool on a wire rack before eating. Sift a dusting of icing sugar over them before serving.

— . —

Gloucester, The Cathedral
The South Porch 1891 28972

Gloucester, Northgate Street 1904 51988

A Taste of GLOUCESTERSHIRE & THE COTSWOLDS

Tetbury, Long Street and the Market House c1965 T155072

The word 'chipping' which appears in many place-names in Gloucestershire and the Cotswolds area, such as Chipping Campden or Chipping Norton, derives from the old Anglo-Saxon word for a market, proving the ancient origins of these places as market centres in the past. It can also be found in street names, such as The Chipping in Tetbury, which was the original site of the market in that town. Tetbury's prosperity grew with the woollen industry during the Middle Ages, and it became an important yarn market. Tetbury was largely undisturbed by the Industrial Revolution, which is why this Cotswold gem retains so many ancient buildings of timeless charm. Built in 1655, Tetbury's Town Hall, or Market House, is one of the grandest of its kind found in the Cotswolds, and for centuries has been at the hub of the town's life and business. On the stone roof, topping the decorative cupola, is a weather vane that features a pair of dolphins. Legend relates that the lord of the manor of Tetbury was sailing across the Irish Sea when his ship was holed and began to sink. After praying that he might be saved, two dolphins appeared and wedged themselves in the hole, thus saving the lord's life.

RECIPE

— . —

Sherry Cake

This rich and boozy fruit cake is another recipe that developed from the fox-hunting heritage of the Cotswolds. It was often served to riders returning home after a long day out in the hunting field.

115g/4oz butter or margarine
115g/4oz caster sugar
3 eggs, separated
225g/8oz plain flour
A pinch of salt
115g/4oz ground almonds
115g/4oz currants
50g/2oz candied mixed peel
50g/2oz glacé cherries, cut into halves
50g/2oz chopped almonds
2 glasses sherry
1 teaspoonful bicarbonate of soda
2 teaspoonfuls vinegar

Pre-heat the oven to 220°C/425°F/Gas Mark 7.

Grease and line a 20cm (8 inch) cake tin. Beat together the butter and sugar until light and fluffy. Add the egg yolks one at a time, beating the mixture well between each addition. Sift the flour and salt into the mixture and gradually stir it in to mix. Stir in the ground almonds, currants, mixed peel, cherries and chopped almonds. Add 1 glass of sherry, and beat the mixture well. Whisk the egg whites until they are stiff and stand in peaks, then fold into the cake mixture, using a large metal spoon. Dissolve the bicarbonate of soda in the vinegar and add to the cake mixture, then beat well. Turn the cake mixture into the prepared cake tin and cover the top with a double layer of greaseproof paper or kitchen foil. Place just below the centre of the pre-heated oven and bake for 10 minutes, then reduce the oven temperature to 160°C/325°F/Gas Mark 3 and bake for a further 2 hours. When the cake is cooked, remove from the oven and carefully pour the other glass of sherry over the cake whilst it is still hot – the sherry will soak into the cake. Leave the cake in the tin to cool before turning out. This cake will keep well, stored in an airtight tin.

— . —

From Stroud, about three miles north of Nailsworth, the Golden Valley starts running eastwards to Sapperton along the River Frome. Chalford is the most remarkable of the villages edged on the valley flanks. The access lanes are so steep and narrow that at one time only donkeys could make the journeys, delivering bread in panniers, or one huge lump of coal on each flank, and the village was often nicknamed 'Neddyshire'. The last baker's donkey was used just before the Second World War, no doubt to the relief of the bakers' boys who had to round up the donkeys from the open common before they could start their deliveries.

Chalford, On the Canal 1910 62711

Chalford, The Village 1910 62713

RECIPE

—·—

Cerney Cake

This fruit cake takes its name from the Cerneys, villages like North and South Cerney which are found along the course of the River Church which flows through the Cotswolds towards the River Thames.

350g/12oz plain flour
175g/6oz caster sugar
175g/6oz butter or margarine, softened to room temperature
115g/4oz mixed dried fruit – currants, raisins, sultanas
1½ teaspoonfuls baking powder
2 eggs, beaten

Pre-heat the oven to 180°C/350°F/Gas Mark 4 (slightly less for a fan oven). Grease and line a cake tin 18-20cms (7-8 inches) in diameter.

Cream together the sugar and the softened butter or margarine until the mixture is light and fluffy. Gradually add in the beaten eggs, a little at the time. Sift together the flour and baking powder and add it to the mixture, then mix in the dried fruit. The mixture will be quite stiff.

Turn the mixture into the prepared cake tin and bake just below the centre of the pre-heated oven for 1 - 1¼ hours, or until a metal skewer inserted into the middle of the cake comes out clean. Leave the cake to cool in the tin for 30 minutes, then turn it out onto a wire rack to cool completely.

—·—

RECIPE

—·—

Cider Cake

The picturesque hillside village of Slad, near Stroud, was immortalised in English literature in Laurie Lee's first novel, 'Cider with Rosie'. Laurie Lee was born in Stroud in 1914 and came to live in Slad when he was three. An account of his childhood years, his book charts the changes in this rural settlement during the 1920s. The title of 'Cider with Rosie' refers to the young Laurie being seduced by Rosie Burdock underneath a hay wagon after drinking cider from a flagon for the first time: 'Never to be forgotten, that first long secret drink of golden fire, juice of those valleys and of that time, wine of wild orchards, of russet summer, of plump red apples ···'. Slad is still much as it was in Laurie Lee's time, and is a place of pilgrimage for admirers of his work. This recipe celebrates his famous book by using cider as an ingredient to make a delicious fruit cake. When making this cake, you will need to remember to soak the dried fruit in the cider overnight.

> 225g/8oz mixed dried fruit – sultanas, raisins and currants
> 4 tablespoonfuls sweet or medium Gloucestershire cider
> 175g/6oz butter or margarine
> 175g/6oz soft brown sugar
> 3 eggs
> 225g/8oz self-raising flour
> 1 teaspoonful mixed spice (optional)

Soak the dried fruit in the cider overnight.

Pre-heat the oven to 180°C/350°F/Gas Mark 4. Grease and line an 18-20cms (7-8 inches) round or square cake tin.

Cream the butter or margarine and add the sugar. Cream again until fluffy. Lightly beat the eggs and gradually beat them into the mixture, a little at a time, adding a little of the flour if necessary to prevent the mixture curdling. Mix in the fruit and cider. Sift the flour and spice together, fold in half of the flour, and mix well, then add the rest of the flour. Turn the mixture into the prepared tin and bake just below the centre of the pre-heated oven for about 1 hour and 15 minutes, until a metal skewer or sharp knife inserted into the cake comes out clean.

—·—

RECIPE

⎯ · ⎯

Gingerbread Husbands

The biscuits usually known as Gingerbread Men were traditionally called Gingerbread Husbands in Gloucestershire. It used to be the custom in many rural parts of the county on Twelfth Night (January 5th, 12 nights after Christmas) to light thirteen fires in honour of Jesus and his twelve apostles, and then immediately stamp out the fire representing Judas, the apostle who betrayed Jesus. Seed cake (flavoured with caraway seeds), plum cake and gingerbread husbands would then be eaten as people stood around the warmth of the remaining twelve fires, and cider would be drunk as the forthcoming harvest was toasted. This should make about 10 biscuits.

225g/8oz self-raising flour
115g/4oz butter or margarine
115g/4oz soft brown sugar
2 teaspoonfuls ground ginger
1 teaspoonful mixed spice
2 level tablespoonfuls golden syrup
1 teaspoonful orange juice
Currants and glacé cherries for decoration
A little icing for decoration, if liked

Pre-heat the oven to 180°C/350°F/Gas Mark 4 and grease two baking trays. Sieve the flour, ginger and mixed spice into a bowl and stir in the sugar. Melt the butter or margarine with the golden syrup in a saucepan, stir in the orange juice, then mix with the flour to form a soft dough. Leave the dough to cool for 30 minutes, when it will have firmed up. Knead the dough lightly, then roll it out on a floured surface to 5mm (¼ inch) thick. Cut out gingerbread men shapes with a special cutter or by cutting round a cardboard shape with a knife. Use a palette knife or frying slice to lift the shapes and place on the baking trays, spaced well apart. Decorate the shapes with currants to form eyes, noses and buttons down their fronts and slices of glacé cherries as mouths, pressing them into the dough. Bake for 12-15 minutes, until firm to the touch and light golden brown, but not burnt around the edges. Remove from the oven and leave on the baking trays for a few minutes to firm up before putting them on a wire tray to cool. If you like, add extra decoration to the shapes with coloured icing.

⎯ · ⎯

Prestbury, A Tram and Cyclists 1907 59051x

A Taste of GLOUCESTERSHIRE & THE COTSWOLDS

Fairford, The Church and the Mill c1950 F145001

St Mary's Church in the village of Fairford is famous for the humorous scenes that are carved on to the church misericords (small lift-up wooden seats). They are believed to date from the time of Henry VII (1457-1509) and show everyday scenes from homes and cookery at that time. One shows a dog watching a pot over the fire, waiting his chance to steal a morsel, while a woman spins; others show two women plucking pigeons for a pie, a wife beating her drunken husband with a ladle, and two men expressing their hunger.

INDEX OF PHOTOGRAPHS

INDEX OF RECIPES

—·—

—·—

FRITH PRODUCTS & SERVICES

Francis Frith would doubtless be pleased to know that the pioneering publishing venture he started in 1860 still continues today. Over a hundred and forty years later, The Francis Frith Collection continues in the same innovative tradition and is now one of the foremost publishers of vintage photographs in the world. Some of the current activities include:

INTERIOR DECORATION

Today Frith's photographs can be seen framed and as giant wall murals in thousands of pubs, restaurants, hotels, banks, retail stores and other public buildings throughout the country. In every case they enhance the unique local atmosphere of the places they depict and provide reminders of gentler days in an increasingly busy and frenetic world.

PRODUCT PROMOTIONS

Frith products are used by many major companies to promote the sales of their own products or to reinforce their own history and heritage. Frith promotions have been used by Hovis bread, Courage beers, Scots Porage Oats, Colman's mustard, Cadbury's foods, Mellow Birds coffee, Dunhill pipe tobacco, Guinness, and Bulmer's Cider.

GENEALOGY AND FAMILY HISTORY

As the interest in family history and roots grows world-wide, more and more people are turning to Frith's photographs of Great Britain for images of the towns, villages and streets where their ancestors lived; and, of course, photographs of the churches and chapels where their ancestors were christened, married and buried are an essential part of every genealogy tree and family album.

FRITH PRODUCTS

All Frith photographs are available Framed or just as Mounted Prints and Posters (size 23 x 16 inches). These may be ordered from the address below. Other products available are - Address Books, Calendars, Jigsaws, Canvas Prints, Postcards and local and prestige books.

THE INTERNET

Already ninety thousand Frith photographs can be viewed and purchased on the internet through the Frith websites and a myriad of partner sites.

For more detailed information on Frith products, look at this site:
www.francisfrith.com

See the complete list of Frith Books at: www.francisfrith.com
This web site is regularly updated with the latest list of publications from The Francis Frith Collection. If you wish to buy books relating to another part of the country that your local bookshop does not stock, you may purchase on-line.

For further information, trade, or author enquiries please contact us at the address below:
The Francis Frith Collection, Unit 6, Oakley Business Park, Wylye Road, Dinton, Wiltshire SP3 5EU.
Tel: +44 (0)1722 716 376 Fax: +44 (0)1722 716 881 Email: sales@francisfrith.co.uk

---

See Frith products on the internet at www.francisfrith.com

FREE PRINT OF YOUR CHOICE
CHOOSE A PHOTOGRAPH FROM THIS BOOK
+ £3.80 POSTAGE

Mounted Print
Overall size 14 x 11 inches (355 x 280mm)

TO RECEIVE YOUR FREE PRINT

Choose any Frith photograph in this book

Simply complete the Voucher opposite and return it with your remittance for £3.50 (to cover postage and handling) and we will print the photograph of your choice in SEPIA (size 11 x 8 inches) and supply it in a cream mount ready to frame (overall size 14 x 11 inches).

Order additional Mounted Prints
at HALF PRICE - £12.00 each (normally £24.00)

If you would like to order more Frith prints from this book, possibly as gifts for friends and family, you can buy them at half price (with no additional postage costs).

Have your Mounted Prints framed

For an extra £20.00 per print you can have your mounted print(s) framed in an elegant polished wood and gilt moulding, overall size 16 x 13 inches (no additional postage required).

IMPORTANT!

❶ Please note: aerial photographs and photographs with a reference number starting with a "Z" are not Frith photographs and cannot be supplied under this offer.

❷ Offer valid for delivery to one UK address only.

❸ These special prices are only available if you use this form to order. You must use the ORIGINAL VOUCHER on this page (no copies permitted). We can only despatch to one UK address.

❹ This offer cannot be combined with any other offer.

As a customer your name & address will be stored by Frith but not sold or rented to third parties. Your data will be used for the purpose of this promotion only.

Send completed Voucher form to:
The Francis Frith Collection,
19 Kingsmead Business Park, Gillingham,
Dorset SP8 5FB

Voucher *for FREE and Reduced Price Frith Prints*

Please do not photocopy this voucher. Only the original is valid, so please fill it in, cut it out and return it to us with your order.

Picture ref no	Page no	Qty	Mounted @ £12.00	Framed + £20.00	Total Cost £
		1	Free of charge*	£	£
			£12.00	£	£
			£12.00	£	£
			£12.00	£	£
			£12.00	£	£
			£12.00	£	£

Please allow 28 days for delivery. Offer available to one UK address only

* Post & handling	£3.80
Total Order Cost	**£**

Title of this book . . . .

I enclose a cheque/postal order for £ . . . .
made payable to 'The Francis Frith Collection'

OR please debit my Mastercard / Visa / Maestro card, details below

Card Number:

Issue No (Maestro only):   Valid from (Maestro):

Card Security Number: Expires:

Signature:

Name Mr/Mrs/Ms . . . .

Address . . . .

. . . .

. . . .

. . . . Postcode . . . .

Daytime Tel No . . . .

Email . . . .

Valid to 31/12/18

Can you help us with information about any of the Frith photographs in this book?

We are gradually compiling an historical record for each of the photographs in the Frith archive. It is always fascinating to find out the names of the people shown in the pictures, as well as insights into the shops, buildings and other features depicted.

If you recognize anyone in the photographs in this book, or if you have information not already included in the author's caption, do let us know. We would love to hear from you, and will try to publish it in future books or articles.

An Invitation from The Francis Frith Collection to Share Your Memories

The 'Share Your Memories' feature of our website allows members of the public to add personal memories relating to the places featured in our photographs, or comment on others already added. Seeing a place from your past can rekindle forgotten or long held memories. Why not visit the website, find photographs of places you know well and add YOUR story for others to read and enjoy? We would love to hear from you!

www.francisfrith.com/memories

Our production team

Frith books are produced by a small dedicated team at offices near Salisbury. Most have worked with the Frith Collection for many years. All have in common one quality: they have a passion for the Frith Collection.

Frith Books and Gifts

We have a wide range of books and gifts available on our website utilising our photographic archive, many of which can be individually personalised.

www.francisfrith.com